Book of Days

CREATE YOUR OWN PRIMITIVE
BOOK FULL OF DAYS

- TO CELEBRATE AND REMEMBER
  LIFE'S SPECIAL OCCASIONS

- RECORD THE YEAR

By Maggie Bonanomi

Book of Days

BY MAGGIE BONANOMI

Editor: Deb Rowden
Designer: Brian Grubb
Photography: Aaron T. Leimkuehler
Illustration: Maggie Bonanomi and Eric Sears
Technical Editor: Kathe Dougherty
Production assistance: Jo Ann Groves

Published by: Kansas City Star Books
1729 Grand Blvd., Kansas City, Missouri,
USA 64108

First edition, first printing • ISBN: 978-1-935362-84-5

Printed in the United States of America by
Walsworth Publishing Co., Marceline, MO

To order copies, call StarInfo at
(816) 234-4636 and say "Books."

KANSAS CITY STAR QUILTS
Continuing the Tradition

PickleDish.com
The Quilter's Home Page
www.PickleDish.com

Dedication

For my hubby, Harold, and my girls,
Heather and Cassandra.

Acknowledgements

Thanks to Doug Weaver and Diane McLendon of
Kansas City Star Books and my team: Deb, Brian
and Aaron and all the others who make everything
look so good. Additional thanks to my editor, Deb
Rowden, for the suggestion that this project could
become a book.

And thanks to my family and friends - without you,
this journey would not be so much fun.

Contents

Months

Introduction

I have always loved books and wanted to make one myself, so I figured out a way to do this. This book, designed to be a Book of Days, is very basic and primitive. It has 25 pages - four per month - with a front page and a back page. The covers are wool-covered cardboard with some appliqué added.

The Book of Days is designed with a non specific year, which can make it a great place to keep a record of important occasions, birthdays and anniversaries. You can use it as you wish – as a journal, a baby book, a memory book to send off with an adult child leaving for college or moving away. Adapt it for your own life or special occasion. You might want it to be a book about quilt projects or rug hooking with photos from guild meetings or rug camps.

I have gathered quotes and verse, used colors I like and photos I have taken. We've included patterns for the designs and quotes and verse to use, but you will need to use your own photos. I have shown you what I did for mine - gather up your own favorite things to photograph. You can use old family pictures to represent that family member's birthday or anniversary – maybe even an old school photo. Instead of photos, you can include bits of old greeting cards, souvenirs, tickets, postcards, seed packets and the like.

The covers are made of wool with some appliqué and cotton covering medium weight chipboard (or 2 layers of cereal/cracker box cardboard). The pages are cardstock. Paper designs on the pages were made by color photocopying: antique fabric, wool, an old deed for the script and the marbleized cover of a book. You need to use copyrighted items carefully (for your personal use only) – that is one reason I used antique fabric. There are wonderful papers available at scrapbooking and hobby shops. Choose things you like, just be sure they go together as you will use them in several combinations throughout the book.

You need to use copyrighted items carefully (for your personal use only)

The pages are bound together with fabric glued along the inside edge of the page, then stitched together in groups called signatures. These groups of pages are then stitched together and covers added to create your book.

Materials Needed

For one 6" x 9" book

These supplies for this project are for the construction of the book as well as designing the pages as I did. Find things you want to use that make this book personal to you.

Fabric

Black wool 9" x 12" for cover

Black cotton 10" x 14" for cover lining

Cotton flannel 9" x 12" to use as batting for cover

Army green wool 3" x 9" for cover binding

Army green wool 5" x 9" wool appliqué for cover stems, leaves, tendril, initials

Greeny blue wool 3" x 6" wool appliqué for cover heart flowers, heart and initial

Yellow green wool scrap wool for appliqué berries

Gauzy muslin (lightweight, loosely woven): 1 yard for binding edges of pages

Note: Maggie dyed her muslin black.

Supplies

1/2" wide black twill tape or ribbon, 26" tie closure

Waxed linen thread - 12" long (for kite in March)

1/2" plum ribbon - 6" long (for March)

12 photos trimmed to 3" x 4"

2 permanent glue sticks (Scotch Brand is good)

Black permanent ink pen, Uniball Vision, .05 waterproof

Small scissors for paper cutting

Craft scissors with deckle edge (optional)

Hand sewing supplies, needle, thread
(my favorite is Coats and Clark summer brown)

Pins and scissors

Ruler

Black Rit dye (to dye the gauzy muslin)

Paper

Sizes available in craft stores are 8 1/2" x 11" and 12" x 12"

Script 11" x 5 1/2"

Marbled brown 9" x 5"

Old shirting 9" x 4"

Brown floral 9" x 4"

Brown check 5" x 6"

Green 9" x 7"

Red 4" x 4"

Plum 3" x 4"

Medium weight chipboard 12" x 12" (you can substitute cereal or cracker box card board - use a double layer)

Black cardstock (100 weight): 13 sheets cut in half to 8 1/2" x 5 1/2" (you will use 25)

10 sheets cream color text weight paper 8 1/2" x 11", for grids for days, verse/quotes

To make a bound book, first prepare the pages for binding. Adding the fabric (black c gauzy muslin) provides a flexible edge so you ca easily flip through the pages. You need 25 - 8 1/: 5 1/2" pages for this project.

Cut the 8 1/2" x 11" cardstock in half so you have 8 1/2" x 5 1/2" pages. Cut 9" x 1 1/4" strips of the muslin to be applied along one 8 1/2" edge of the page (the inside edge). Use a permanent gluestic apply glue along the 8 1/2" edge.

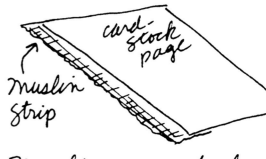

Lay the 9" x 1 1/4" strip on the glued area, leaving slightly more than half the width off the edge of t paper. Fold the muslin over and glue it along the edge to secure the muslin, trim. Leave a little edg the fold loose, this will be where you stitch your p together.

Putting Together the Pages

‹ 5 pages and whipstitch them together - this
p of pages is called a signature. Repeat with 4 more
les. Now stack these 5 signatures and whipstitch
together. Do so loosely enough so you can freely
he pages.

glue

*muslin folded over to front.
glued in place*

muslin

*muslin strip
glued to both sides of
page, leaving slight
overhang - maybe 1 or 2 threads worth.*

e you have the pages bound,
ead and decorate your pages.
ing the pages together
helps you keep the pages
der.

*stitch 5 pages together thru muslin
edge this makes "1 signature"*

Resources

Cardstock and text paper: www. frenchpaper.com
($50 minimum order)

Gauzy muslin: www.quiltersstation.com

Gauzy muslin: www.sgcountrysampler.com

Papers for cutouts: scrapbook and hobby stores

Chipboard: hobby and art stores

Black permanent ink pen: craft or office supply

The Beginning and the End

I started the front page with a wonderful quote I have always loved, along with a sprig, leaves, and seeds cut from script paper, and heart buds from marbleized paper. The last page has a marbleized paper heart along with the words "The end " and then your initials cut from whatever paper you wish.

I use four grids per month to list the dates. Each grid has seven lines plus a narrow one. Most times the narrow one is at the top with a bit of drawing or words, but occasionally I reverse it so the narrow line is at the bottom. I added my drawings for each month to inspire you - you may use them or not.

Art for the beginning and the end of the book is found on page 32.

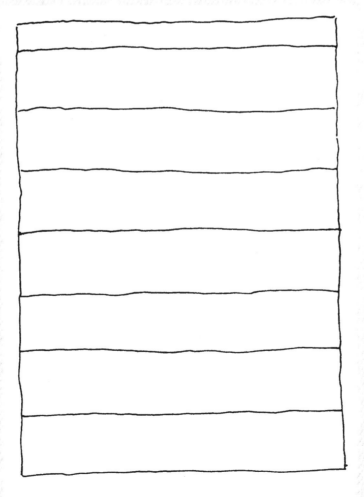

this is the layout for a week - you need 4 per month - extra days can be added

Book Covers

The covers for the book of days are constructed individually then attached to the bound pages. I suggest you appliqué the wool covers before stitching them in place.

For the covers you need:

2 each 5 3/4" x 9" chipboard

2 each 5 3/4" x 9" cotton flannel for thin batting

2 each 5 3/4" x 9" antique black wool

2 each 6 3/4" x 10" cotton for inside cover

Needle and thread to sew the covers together

Twill tape

The wool for the covers should be the same size as the chipboard. Use the pattern pieces on the next page to cut out the design adding the vine c from Army green wool.

Other fabric measurements:

See list at top of next page.

The three heart buds are cut from old greeny blu wool and the berries are from mustard wool. Re to the photo on the next page for the placement of the appliqué and stitch in place. I originally planned this for the front cover, and the heart cu from the same old greeny blue wool and initials from scrap wool for the back cover. While fitting the covers in place, I reversed them and decided preferred the simple cover for the front so I wen ahead and stitched them in place. Before we get

...ver templates

top heart

middle heart

main stem 8" x ¼"
side stems 2¼" x ⅛"
1½" x ⅛"
tendril 8" x ⅛"

bottom heart

right leaf cut 1

⑤ berries

cut initials from scrap wool

top leaf cut 2

left leaf cut 1

...at point, construct your covers.
...initial measures 2 1/2" x 2".

...nstructing the covers

...a gluestick and tack the cotton flannel
...ing) onto what will be the inside of each
...board cover. The flannel I use usually has one
...with a flannel nap, the other side is more like
...lar cotton.
...lown a 6 3/4" x 10" cotton piece, right side
...n. Place the chipboard on top, fabric sides
...ther. Run the gluestick around the edges of the top
...e chipboard and bring up the raw edges of the cotton
...c onto the surface, gluing it in place. Lay the appliquéd wool right side up
...the chipboard covering the fabric edges. Whipstitch it in place. Repeat for
...econd cover.

...aching the covers

...tach the cover, lay the cover on top of the bound pages and stitch it in place
...g the bound edge (don't stitch so tightly that you cannot flip the cover open).
...at for the back cover. Cut the twill tape or ribbon pieces: one 12" for the
...t and one 14" for the back. Stitch the twill ties or ribbons in place along the
...d edge at the center.

...ding the covers

...cover binding is a strip of Army green wool 3" x 9". Center this on the back,
...apping each cover's bound edge about 1/2" - 3/4". Whipstitch it to the covers.

Front and back covers

January

Page 1. The year begins and - for some of us - it is winter time. The letters *January* are cut from marbleized paper; there are shirting icicles hanging from the grid sheet.

2. When I think of January, I think of white things and the calm after the busy colorful holiday season. For my photo, I gathered up white buttons, ironstone and old white painted turnings from an old porch.

3. Snow and a snowman fit naturally here. The letters were cut from brown floral, brown check and old shirting paper. The snowman and snowflakes are from shirting as well, with nose and arms of marbleized paper.

4. Cut the snowflake from shirting paper and add the words *blow, blow thou winter wind.*

Follow Maggie's tips for pages 1 to 4, left to right

February

Page 1. This is often thought of as the Valentine or heart month so that's my theme. The month is abbreviated; the letters are cut from script with a brown checked arrow underneath.

2. For my photo I gathered up some old tin baking items: heart cake pans and cookie cutters, as well as a few fluted pans and stacked them in a wood box. I love old dark tins.

3. The heart is cut from red paper and the background is green. I added dash marks to represent stitching

4. I love this verse from Proverbs. Don't forget to leave a spot for Leap year!

FEB

arrow ends

Hearts

proverbs 15:15

He that is of a merry heart hath a continual feast.

Valentine's Day!   take a leap!

March

Page 1. This month is known for its windy days and kite flying. My kite is cut from script paper, the lines and tail are from waxed linen thread. Hang the tag with March on the tail and add 5 assorted bows.

2. The green eggs were the inspiration for this photo. I got them from a local farmer. The colors were so spring-like, I added a few nests, some ribbon, crocheted edging, and a few buttons in a large ironstone bowl.

3. You cannot go wrong with this verse from the Song of Solomon. I cut it out with deckle-edge scissors and added a piece of plum ribbon.

4. Here are a few new flowers, cut from plum and green paper, adding the center and stamen from script paper.

For lo, the winter is past; the rain is over & gone; The flowers appear on the earth...
~ Song of Solomon 2:10-12

come gentle spring, come

15.	
16.	
17.	
18.	
19.	
20.	
21.	

grow, grow, grow, grow

22.			
23.			
24.			
25.			
26.		29.	
27.		30.	
28.		31.	

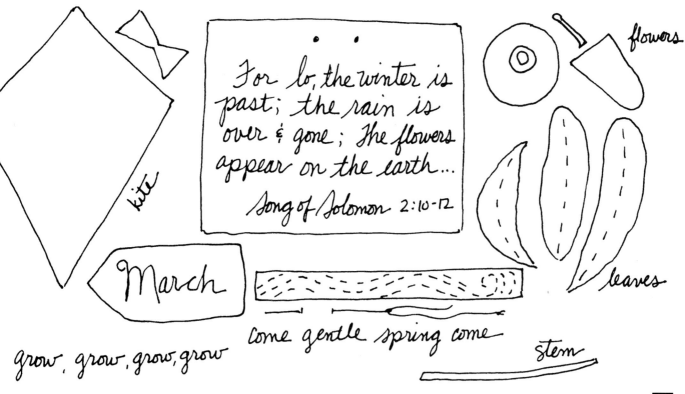

kite

For lo, the winter is past; the rain is over & gone; The flowers appear on the earth...
Song of Solomon 2:10-12

flowers

March

come gentle spring come

leaves

grow, grow, grow, grow

stem

April

Page 1. For April showers... a green umbrella with plum paper letters, a handle cut from marbleized paper.

2. This photo was taken when the local lilacs were in full bloom - there was a wonderful old bush that had these incredible blossoms. I filled some ironstone pitchers and added a few other items...I think I can still smell their fragrance.

3. A daffodil of script paper with green stem and leaf along with the exclamation of '*In spring the earth awakens*' cut out with deckle-edge scissors.

4. A nest is natural, one egg is from script paper and one from shirting. The nest of marbleized and brown check paper sits upon a branch of brown floral and green leaves.

In spring the earth awakens!

Bloom where you are planted.

15.
16
17.
18.
19
20.
21.

22.
23.
24.
25.
26.
27.   29
28.   30

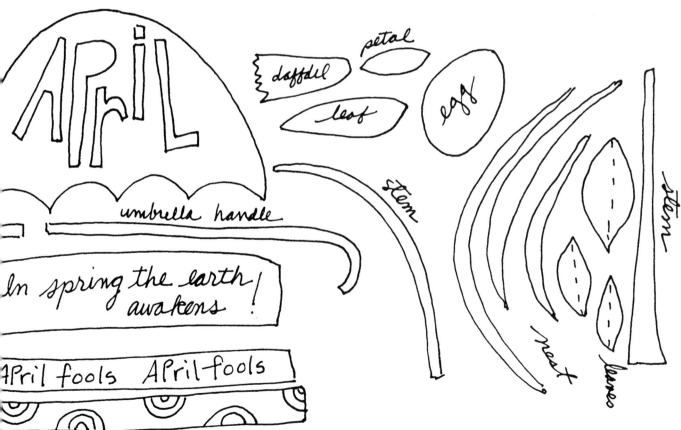

APRIL

petal
daffdil
leaf
egg
stem
stem
nest
leaves

umbrella handle

In spring the earth
awakens!

April fools   April fools

bloom where you are planted.

May

Page 1. I remember construction paper May baskets filled with candy and flowers, left anonymously on the doorstep with a ringing of the doorbell. Here is a little May basket cut from script paper, trimmed in brown check. Add a plum bow and the month of May banner.

2. For my photo I gathered some favorite old sewing items - a pincushion, spools of thread, buttons and bits of fabric.

3. To attract bees in the garden you need a bee hive. This one is cut from script paper sitting on green grass. The bees are of brown check with shirting wings - I think I hear them buzzing!

4. I love this Shakespeare quote.

May day Bzzzz

Full many a
glorious morning
have I seen ~
~ Shakespeare

Basket

rim

base

May

grass base

hive

grasses

3 Bees

6 wings

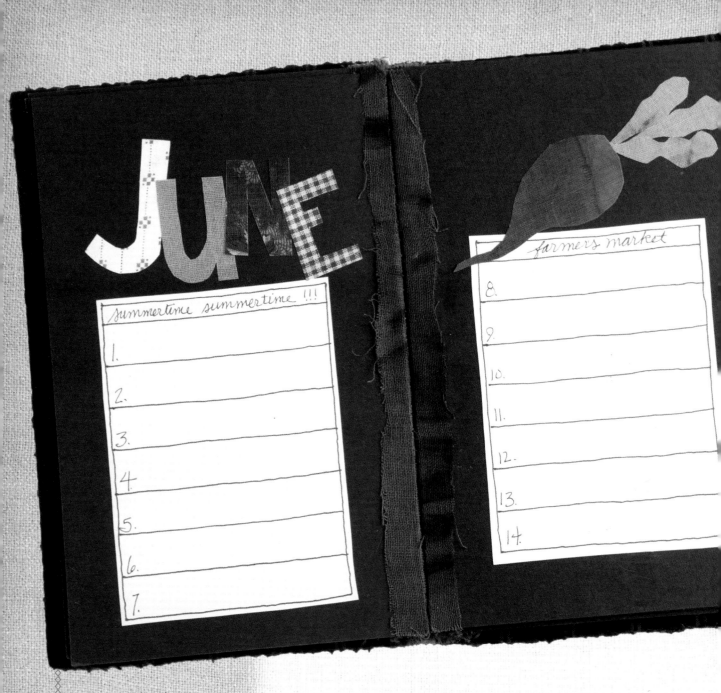

June

Page 1. The letters spelling June are cut from shirting, green, brown floral, and brown check paper.

2. The beet fresh from the farmers market is cut from plum paper with green leaves.

3. My photo is a gathering of things I love - old books, a few nature items and a small portrait. Summer is a great time for a good read.

4. Henry David Thoreau always says it right.

read a good book.

15.

16.

17.

18.

19.

20

21.

22.

23

24.

25.

26.

27.   29

28.   30.

"You must taste the first glass of a days nectar if you would get all the Spirit of it" ~ Thoreau

UNE

beet

leaf
cut 3

summertime summertime!!
farmers market
read a good book

"You must taste the first glass of a days nectar if you would get all the spirit of it" ~ Thoreau

July

Page 1. A cool slice of watermelon starts this month. Use red and green paper to make a nice slice. Add a few black or dark brown seeds and the little banner with *July* written on it.

2. Flags are very fitting this month. For my photo I gathered tiny silk flags I found years ago into a tiny crock. Add a star cut from script paper.

3. Add a little drawing with a flag and *Hooray for the Red, White and Blue.*

4. End the month with a little pot of flowers for your windowsill. The pot is marbleized paper, leaves are green, blooms from brown check, red and brown floral with little scraps for centers.

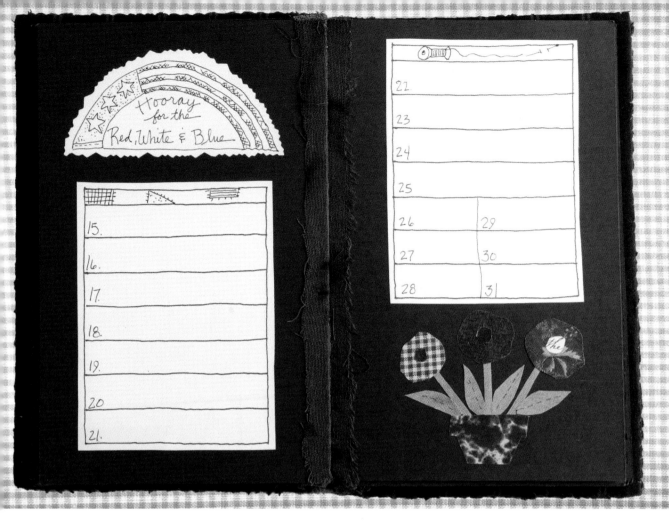

stem

leaf

flower

ANTS...

JULY

America the beautiful !

Hooray
for the
Red, White & Blue

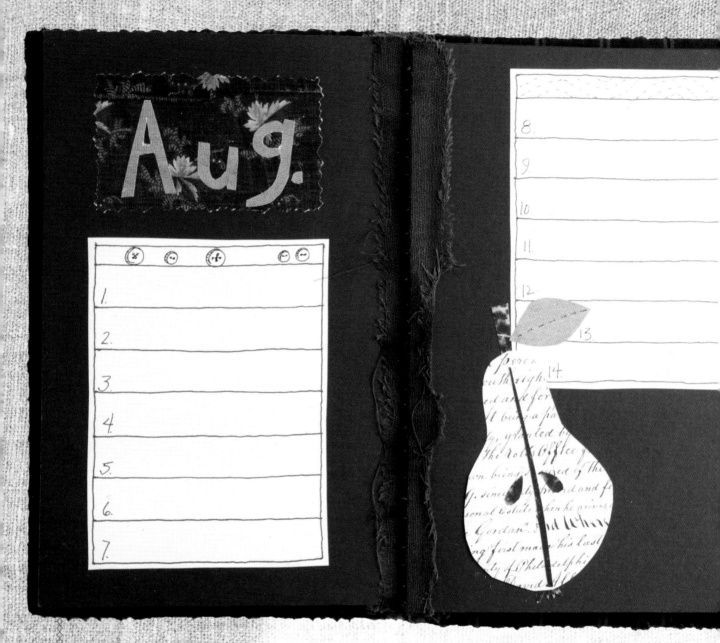

August

Page 1. Start the month with *Aug.* cut from green paper, set upon a backing of brown floral.

2. I love the shape of pears. This one is cut from script paper with core, seeds, stem and blossom end from marbleized paper.

3. For my photo, I gathered some of my collection of stone fruit along with a goofy bunch of pink velvet grapes that my daughter gave me. (These may have graced a hat once.) I set them in an old tin strainer.

4. Again, Thoreau says all the right things.

stone fruit

15.
16.
17.
18.
19.
20.
21.

22.
23.
24.
25.
26.   29
27.   30
28.   31

Live in each season as it
passes. Breathe the air,
drink the drink, taste the
fruit and resign yourself
to the influences of each.
~ Thoreau

Aug.

stone fruit

Live in each season as it
passes. Breathe the air
drink the drink, taste the
fruit and resign yourself
to the influences of each.
~ Thoreau

Home comforts

8.

9.

10.

11.

12.

13.

14.

Sept.

1.

2.

3.

4.

5.

6.

7.

September

Page 1.   A little quilt block, the nine patch is one of my favorites. Use brown check and brown floral and a few dashes for stitches - it gives the Sept. banner a special look.

2. This photo was a combination of antique bedding, a blue and white quilt, a red wool coverlet and a sheet with crocheted edging, along with an old Shaker box.

3. Corn on the cob is a delicious treat. Here the corn is brown check, silk from script, and husks from green paper.

4. This time Whittier has the right words.

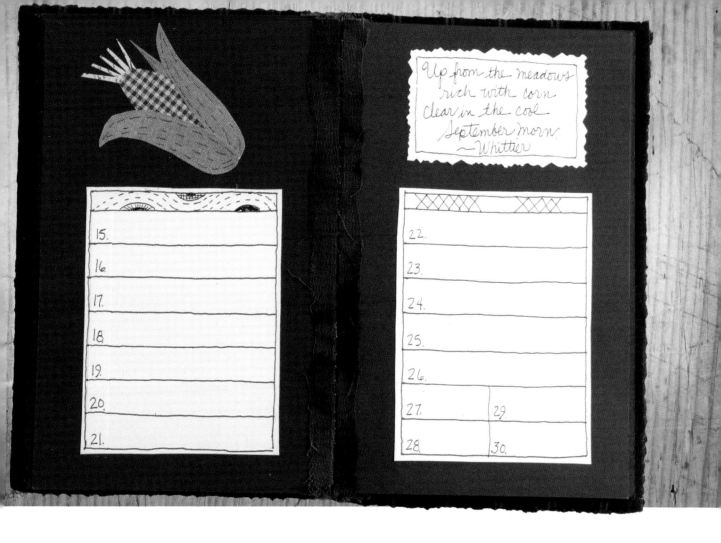

Up from the meadows
rich with corn
clear in the cool
September morn.
~Whittier

15.	
16.	
17.	
18.	
19.	
20.	
21.	

22.	
23.	
24.	
25.	
26.	
27.	29.
28.	30.

Sept

Up from the meadows
rich with corn
clear in the cool
September morn.
~Whittier

Home Comforts

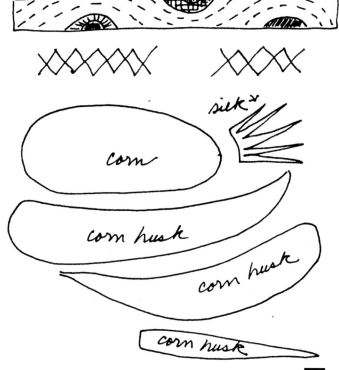

sick *

corn

corn husk

corn husk

corn husk

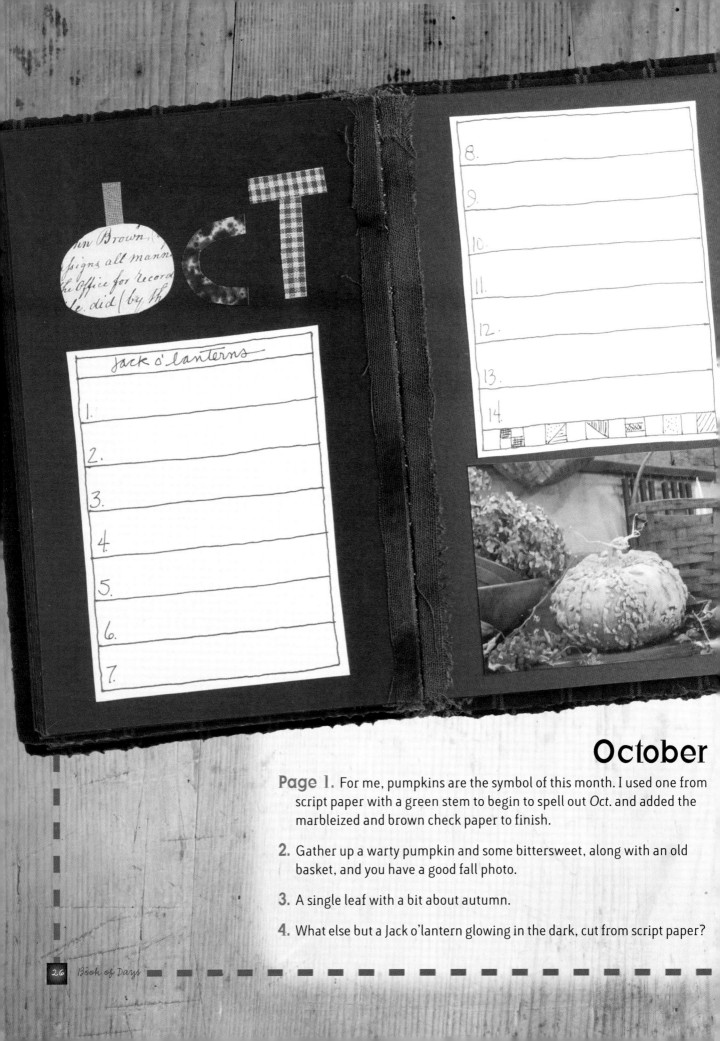

Jack o'lanterns

1.
2.
3.
4.
5.
6.
7.

8.
9.
10.
11.
12.
13.
14.

October

Page 1. For me, pumpkins are the symbol of this month. I used one from script paper with a green stem to begin to spell out *Oct.* and added the marbleized and brown check paper to finish.

2. Gather up a warty pumpkin and some bittersweet, along with an old basket, and you have a good fall photo.

3. A single leaf with a bit about autumn.

4. What else but a Jack o'lantern glowing in the dark, cut from script paper?

November

Page 1. These letters are cut from brown floral on a green background. Add a twisted vine from marbleized paper and some berries from brown check.

2. This photo is again part of a collection that was on my mantle: old black tin boxes, old books and some berries.

3. I love this old hymn. Since Thanksgiving comes in November, it seems appropriate to me.

4. A few leaves - one from brown floral paper and one from script papers - are perfect for this big green and brown checked acorn.

For the beauty of the earth
for the beauty of the sky
for the love which from our
birth, over and around us
lie. Lord of all to Thee
we pray, this our gift of
grateful praise
— old hymn

Be Ye Thankful

15.
16.
17.
18.
19.
20.
21.

acorns & oak leaves

22.
23.
24.
25.
26.
27.   29.
28.   30.

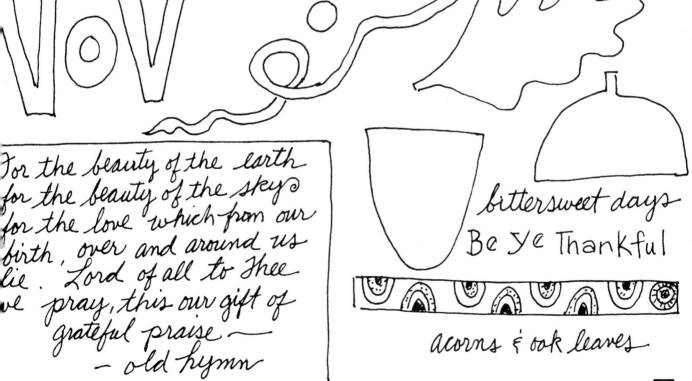

NoV

For the beauty of the earth
for the beauty of the sky
for the love which from our
birth, over and around us
lie. Lord of all to Thee
we pray, this our gift of
grateful praise —
— old hymn

bittersweet days
Be Ye Thankful

acorns & oak leaves

Somehow not only this season, But all the year thru ~ The joy that you give to others ~ Is the joy that comes back to you.

let it snow!

1.
2.
3.
4.
5.
6.
7.

holly berries

8.
9.
10.
11.
12.
13.
14.

December

Page 1. A red and green mitten-covered hand with a calling card for *Dec.* starts off this month.

2. A sprig of holly cut from script paper, with leaves of brown floral and brown checked, and some red berries cover one side of the grid. The verse sums it all up perfectly.

3. Old and new silver ornaments are one of my favorite Christmas decorations. These were piled into a box after I took them off my tree, I just thought it looked good.

4. The clock and hand seems to represent the passing of one year into another - the clock is cut from script paper and the hands are slivers of marbleized paper. I love the saying on the hand.